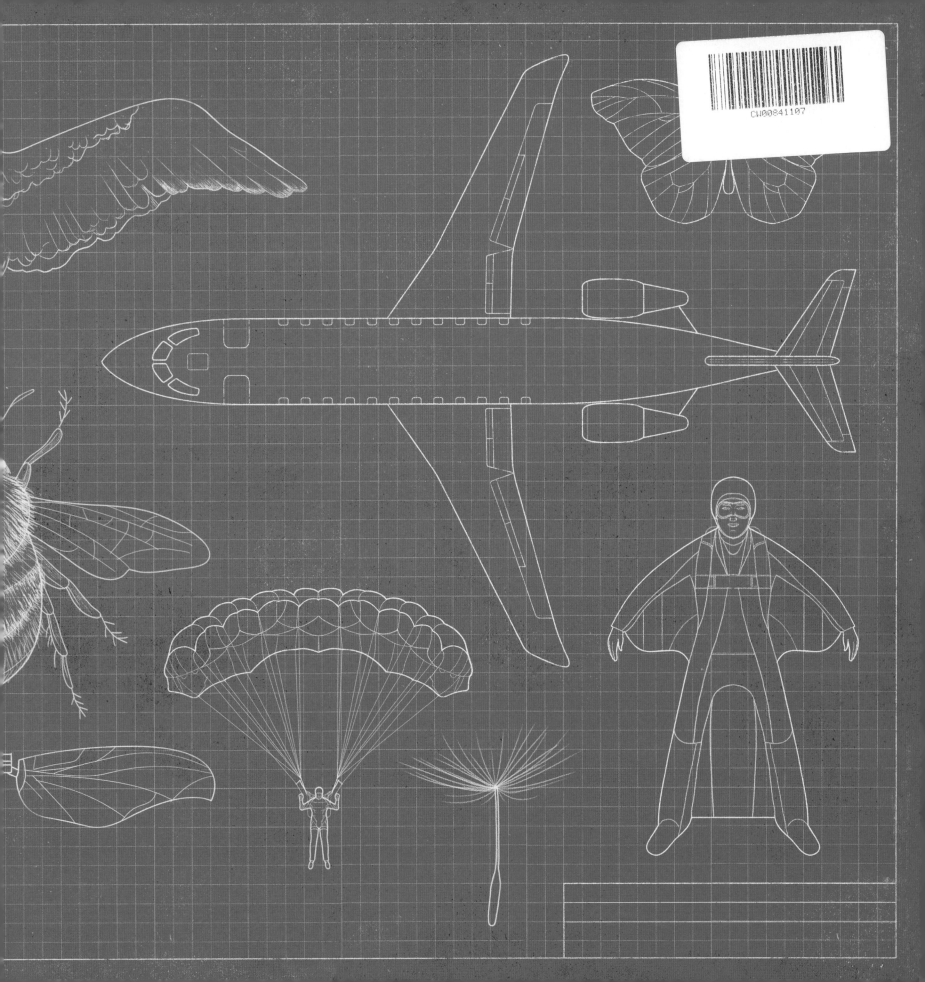

IN THE SKY
DESIGNS INSPIRED BY NATURE

For Adriana, whose curiosity flies
higher than a plane.
- G.V.

360 DEGREES

An imprint of the Little Tiger Group

www.littletiger.co.uk

1 Coda Studios, 189 Munster Road, London SW6 6AW

First published in Great Britain 2020 by Caterpillar Books Ltd

Text by Harriet Evans

Text copyright © Caterpillar Books Ltd 2020

Illustrations copyright © Gonçalo Viana 2020

A CIP Catalogue record for this book is available from the British Library

All rights reserved • ISBN: 978-1-84857-940-8

Printed in China • CPB/2700/1345/1219

10 9 8 7 6 5 4 3 2 1

IN THE SKY
DESIGNS INSPIRED BY NATURE

Harriet Evans   Gonçalo Viana

LiTTLE TiGER
LONDON

Contents

Time for Take-off...

Scientists take inspiration from nature because plants and animals evolve over millions of years. Some creatures become extinct, but successful species continuously adapt and improve. Since we can't hope to test our own inventions this thoroughly, why not let nature do the work?

This book shows how the creatures that fly through the air and the trees that stretch towards the sky have led to some of our best machines. From our first forays into flight to lightning-fast internet, much of today's technology has its roots in wildlife. Get a bird's-eye view of different topics and flick to the glossary at the back for help with some of the harder concepts. Read on and discover that the sky's the limit!

(400–200 BCE)

Chinese kites

Chinese kites were one of humanity's earliest attempts to copy bird flight.

(1452–1519)

Leonardo da Vinci

Italian painter Leonardo da Vinci designed ornithopters — flying machines with flapping wings. Sadly, da Vinci realised these vehicles would never work if they were actually made.

(1853)

George Cayley

English inventor George Cayley created the first glider to carry a person. After Cayley's coachman was forced to test the contraption, he apparently resigned, saying he was hired to drive, not to fly!

Plane Talking

For thousands of years humans have looked up to the sky for inspiration. We've built aircraft to imitate birds since 400 BCE and even now engineers are learning from the natural world.

(1903)

The Wright brothers

Partly inspired by pigeons, the American brothers Orville and Wilbur Wright designed and flew the first successful aeroplane.

Did you know?

A sheep, a cockerel and a duck float up over Versailles in France. No, that isn't the beginning of a joke but a test flight for Joseph-Michel and Jacques-Étienne Montgolfier's hot-air balloon invention in 1783.

The first passenger planes were created in the 1910s but flying only became more widely affordable in 1950s America.

(The future)

Lockheed Stratoliner

The Lockheed Stratoliner is based on the bar-tailed godwit, the bird that holds the record for the longest non-stop flight, from Alaska to Australia. Though only at design stage, this plane may one day complete similarly long journeys without refuelling.

(2013)

The Airbus A350 XWB

The Airbus A350 XWB has curved wingtips like a bird to help it fly faster.

(1969)

Concorde

Concorde was the first passenger plane to fly faster than the speed of sound (1,235kmph or 767mph).

(1914–18 and 1939–45)

World Wars

During the World Wars, technology improved dramatically! Planes became faster and more adept at manoeuvring.

Fly Like a Bird

Your body moves and stays still because of pushes and pulls called forces. These impact everything in the world and even the creatures and machines soaring above it! Anything flying straight at a constant speed is affected by these forces:

Lift is pushing it up.

Air resistance, also known as drag, is forcing it back.

Thrust is pushing it forward.

Weight is pulling it down.

Under nature's wing

Many aeroplane wings are curved like those of a bird so that when air flows over them it is directed downwards, which in turn pushes the wing up, creating lift. The faster the object and air are moving past each other, the greater the lift.

Air directed downwards

Smooth move

One of the reasons birds smooth their feathers is to become more streamlined, allowing air particles to flow quickly past them for faster flight. Similarly, aeroplanes are made from smooth metal to reduce drag. They also stow their wheels and other landing gear during flight, just as birds tuck their feet into their bodies when flying.

Smooth feathers

Tucked-in feet

V is for V-shaped formation

Assume positions! Birds travel in a V formation to save energy. As they fly, their wings push air upwards. This is called upwash. Birds at the back of the group can coast on the upwash of the birds in front and use it for lift. The birds swap positions so that none of the group gets too tired.

Air forces across the world already fly in V formations but scientists in America are looking at whether other aeroplanes could follow suit.

Bird Big Shots

BOOM! In 1990 the Shinkansen bullet train sounded like a gunshot as it blasted out of tunnels across Japan at around 210kmph (130mph). Luckily, engineer Eiji Nakatsu was a keen bird watcher and he looked to his feathery friends for a solution to the noise...

Train of thought

As the train sped along, it transferred some of its energy to the air as sound. To reduce the noise, Nakatsu had to make the train more streamlined, especially the device connecting the train to overhead wires, called the pantograph.

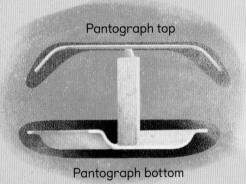

Pantograph top

Pantograph bottom

Letting it slide

Nakatsu took inspiration from the Adélie penguin for the bottom half of the pantograph. The penguin's smooth body helps it slide through snow and water quickly and quietly.

Owl right now

Nakatsu used the shape of owl wings for the top half of the pantograph because owls are so streamlined that they are almost silent when they fly.

Regal features

The kingfisher dives into water to catch fish. It has to be streamlined to dive into deep, dense water and its smooth, pointy beak is the perfect tool to pierce the surface of rivers and lakes. Nakatsu copied this shape for the front of the bullet train, which stopped the vehicle making such a loud noise when it exited tunnels.

Since they began running in 1964, Japanese bullet trains have carried over 10 billion passengers!

Bullet trains are getting faster and faster! They can now reach speeds in excess of 320kmph (199mph).

To Infinity and Beyond

Planes and trains aren't the only vehicles inspired by creatures of the sky. Nature's flyers have helped us sail the oceans and could even hold the key to exploring the depths of space.

Marsbees

When David Bowie sang 'Is there life on Mars?', he probably didn't think the answer might involve space bees. NASA is developing small insect-like robots to send to Mars to look for methane, a gas that some living creatures emit. With bumblebee-sized bodies and wings like cicadas', these new robots would be much faster than the space rovers currently used.

Wingsuits and flying squirrels

Flying squirrels have flaps of skin joining their wrists and ankles, which they extend to help them glide between trees. Their shape increases their drag, slowing them down as gravity pulls them towards the ground. Similarly, wingsuits have inflated fabric between the legs and under the arms to slow wearers down once they leap out of aeroplanes or BASE jump.

Parachutes and dandelion seeds

Using their bristles to create a ring-shaped bubble of air above them, dandelion seeds can float over 1km (0.6mi) before they land. This type of parachute wouldn't work for people – we're much too heavy! Instead, researchers are looking to copy dandelions to create eco-friendly drones that glide on the wind.

Sails and wings

Sails act a bit like vertical wings – they direct air over their curved surfaces.

Helicopters and hummingbirds

Hummingbirds flap their wings at up to 80 beats a second to hover mid-flight and sip from flowers. These brilliant birds supposedly inspired Igor Sikorsky, the inventor of the helicopter.

Tree-mendous Buildings

Cities are sometimes called concrete jungles, full of buildings that stretch up into the sky jostling for light and space. Though you might not see monkeys swinging from roof to roof any time soon, buildings have a lot more in common with trees than you might think. Here are some of the ways architects have taken a leaf from nature's book.

Branching out

Dougong brackets are interlacing pieces of wood that help pillars hold up roofs in traditional Chinese architecture. The shape of a bracket is similar to the branch of a tree; both are superb at bearing weight and withstanding natural forces. In fact, one pagoda with dougong brackets has remained standing since 1056, surviving several earthquakes!

Dougong brackets

Is it a tree? Is it a building?

...No, it's a Supertree!

Supertrees have been built in Singapore. Standing at 25–50m (182–164ft) tall, they are described as 'vertical gardens' and their steel 'trunks' are covered with foliage. They collect rainwater just as real trees absorb moisture, and some are even fitted with solar panels to convert sunlight into energy.

Sunny side up

Trees spread their leaves out so that they can receive as much sunlight as possible. An apartment building in France called Arbre Blanc ('white tree') mimics this leaf arrangement with its balconies to make the most of available light and space.

Photosynthesis

Trees are important because their leaves create oxygen in a process called photosynthesis.

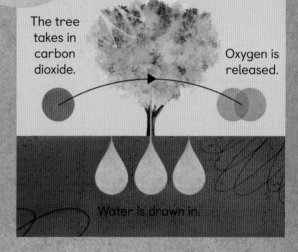

The leaves absorb light energy, which is needed for this reaction.

After the carbon dioxide and water react with the help of sunlight, sugar is formed. This gives the tree energy.

The tree takes in carbon dioxide.

Oxygen is released.

Water is drawn in.

Treehouses

Vietnamese architects have covered the roofs of some houses with trees. Trees can lower the temperature of an area and improve the air quality.

15

Hive Homes and Window Webs

Despite their tiny size, insects can help us with our building projects, providing clever solutions to difficult problems. Here are a couple of ways we can be brainy like bees and smart like spiders.

Sweeter than honey

Bees are brilliant builders, creating hives from hexagonal cells made of waxy honeycomb. These shapes fit together easily and while the cell walls are made from relatively little wax, they have a large amount of storage space for honey and larvae. Because hexagons use space so efficiently, we've borrowed this shape for many of our own designs...

The Sinosteel skyscraper in Tianjin, China, will have six-sided windows to help regulate heat and light.

British company HiveHaus builds homes with hexagonal rooms that slot together so that it's easy to make the house larger or smaller.

In Izola, Slovenia, social housing has been built in hexagonal modules to create shade and offer privacy.

What a pane!

The last thing a spider wants is for a bird to fly through its carefully woven web. To prevent such a catastrophe, certain species, such as the orb weaver, have evolved to spin silk that birds can spot. These webs reflect ultraviolet light, a special type of radiation that birds can see but humans can't.

Since it is estimated that millions of birds die every year from window collisions, German scientists have created a glass that reflects ultraviolet in the same way. Not too bird-brained!

Notable places that use this glass include the Bronx Zoo in New York.

Green Machines

From whizzing wind turbines to sleek solar panels, there are plenty of ways to power our planet without hurting it. Instead of using fossil fuels, we should follow nature's lead. Who wouldn't want to run on sunshine?

Did you know?

American scientists are developing 'artificial leaves' that use energy from sunlight to create fuels from water and carbon dioxide.

Photosynthesis

Carbon dioxide

Sunlight

Oxygen

Sugar

Water

Tree treats

Trees and plants come complete with their very own sugar factories to give them energy. In a process called photosynthesis, plants combine carbon dioxide, which they breathe in through their leaves, and water that they slurp up through their roots. With the help of sunlight, the end result is sugar and oxygen – delicious!

Hot topic

The Swiss scientist Michael Grätzel designs solar panels inspired by chlorophyll - the special substance in plants that harnesses the Sun's energy. Compared to typical solar panels, Grätzel's versions work better in dim light. They are made with titania, an ingredient in toothpaste. It's now keeping our planet squeaky clean as well as our teeth!

It's a breeze

Palm trees are warriors against the wind with leaves that bend along their spines to reduce the area that air can buffet. In America, scientists have designed wind turbines with blades that bunch together like these leaves, folding inwards to follow the wind's direction. These designs would allow for taller wind turbines that could produce ten times as much energy as those currently used in the US!

Light Bulb Moment

Before electricity, light bulbs, LEDs and
neon lights came the humble firefly.
We might think we outshine these
gently glowing creatures, but
they can still shed light on
how we live...

Hot stuff

The light that fireflies emit is a
type of bioluminescence. It's created
naturally by a reaction between oxygen
and chemicals found inside a firefly's
abdomen. Almost 100% of the energy in
this reaction becomes light while some light bulbs
are only around 10% as efficient, losing most
of their energy as heat.

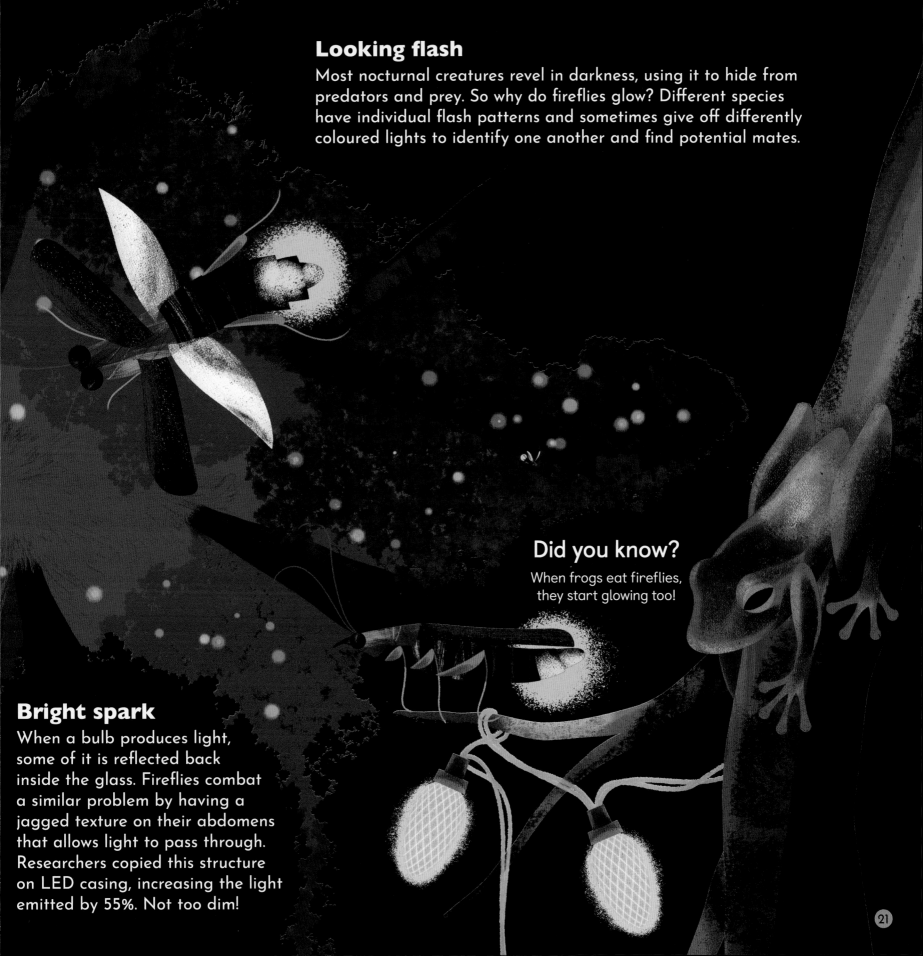

Looking flash

Most nocturnal creatures revel in darkness, using it to hide from predators and prey. So why do fireflies glow? Different species have individual flash patterns and sometimes give off differently coloured lights to identify one another and find potential mates.

Did you know?

When frogs eat fireflies, they start glowing too!

Bright spark

When a bulb produces light, some of it is reflected back inside the glass. Fireflies combat a similar problem by having a jagged texture on their abdomens that allows light to pass through. Researchers copied this structure on LED casing, increasing the light emitted by 55%. Not too dim!

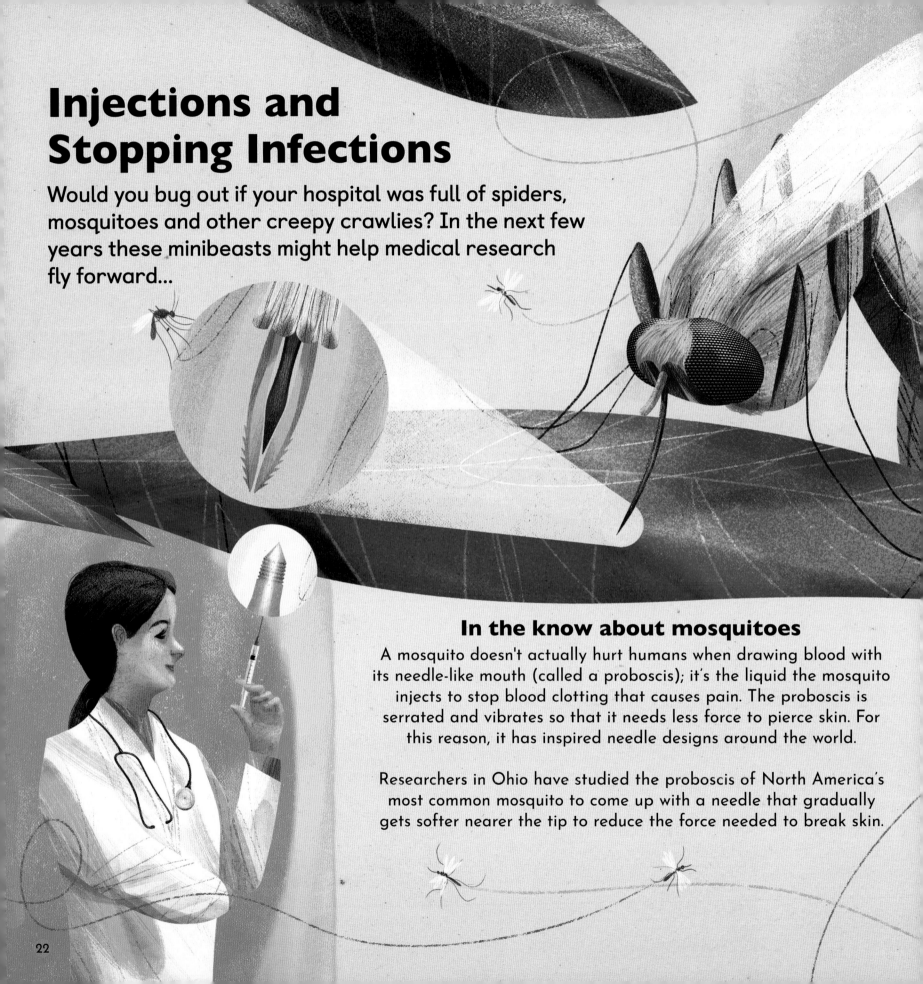

Injections and Stopping Infections

Would you bug out if your hospital was full of spiders, mosquitoes and other creepy crawlies? In the next few years these minibeasts might help medical research fly forward...

In the know about mosquitoes

A mosquito doesn't actually hurt humans when drawing blood with its needle-like mouth (called a proboscis); it's the liquid the mosquito injects to stop blood clotting that causes pain. The proboscis is serrated and vibrates so that it needs less force to pierce skin. For this reason, it has inspired needle designs around the world.

Researchers in Ohio have studied the proboscis of North America's most common mosquito to come up with a needle that gradually gets softer nearer the tip to reduce the force needed to break skin.

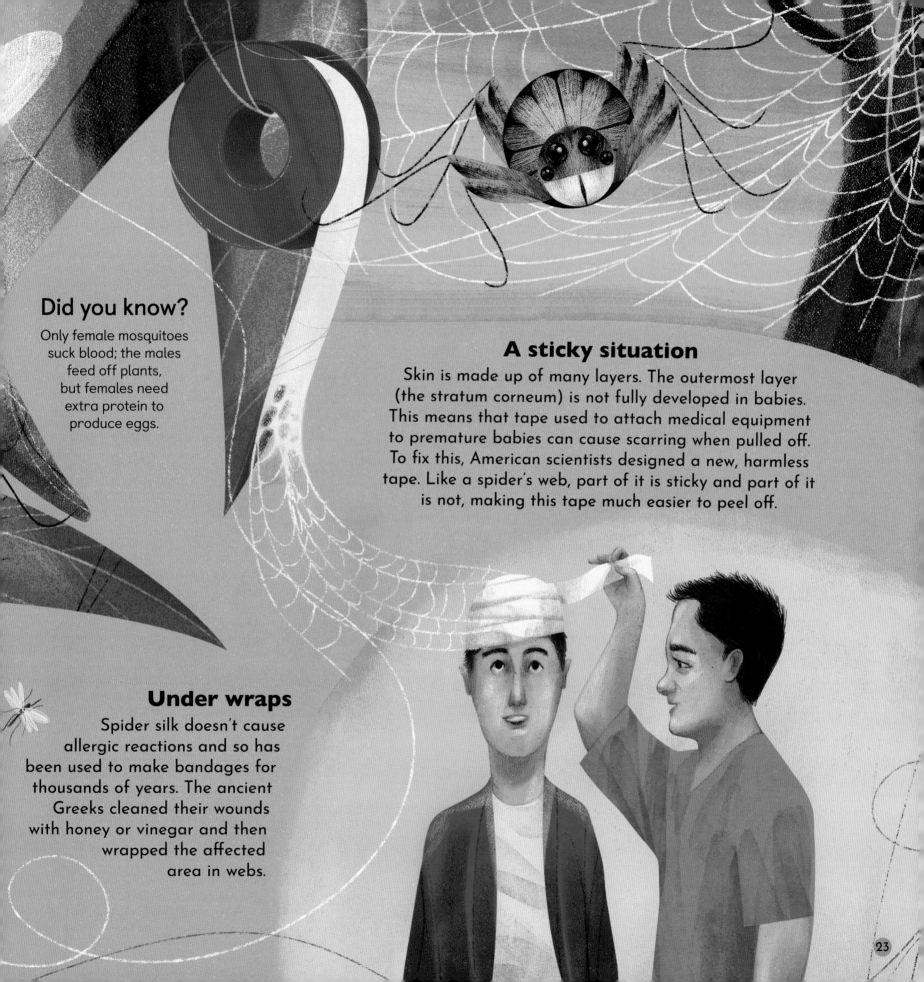

Did you know?

Only female mosquitoes suck blood; the males feed off plants, but females need extra protein to produce eggs.

A sticky situation

Skin is made up of many layers. The outermost layer (the stratum corneum) is not fully developed in babies. This means that tape used to attach medical equipment to premature babies can cause scarring when pulled off. To fix this, American scientists designed a new, harmless tape. Like a spider's web, part of it is sticky and part of it is not, making this tape much easier to peel off.

Under wraps

Spider silk doesn't cause allergic reactions and so has been used to make bandages for thousands of years. The ancient Greeks cleaned their wounds with honey or vinegar and then wrapped the affected area in webs.

What's the Big Eye-dea?

With their large eyes, insects can help us
see in weird and wonderful ways. Moths,
especially, are providing insight to scientists...

In the dark

Flying under the cover of night, moths avoid becoming
snacks for passing birds and bats because they have a
special rough coating on their eyes that drinks in light
without reflecting it.

By including microscopic bumps on the surface of
electronic devices, scientists have copied this coating
to create anti-reflective phone screens that give
off less glare in direct sunlight.

The structure has also been used for solar panels,
because these need to absorb as much light as
possible to generate the greatest amount of energy.

Like a moth to a (camera) frame

Moths have excellent vision and their eyes inspired the NASA camera that records heat, otherwise known as infrared light, from space. The infrared signal is very weak when it reaches us so as much of it needs to be captured as possible. Indirectly, moth eyes have helped us see stars forming and the black hole at the centre of our galaxy!

Insects vs humans

It might not seem like a fair fight between insect and human vision; while we have two eyes, some insects have compound eyes, made up of thousands of small units called ommatidia that all look in different directions.

Ommatidia allow insects to see a large area. Dragonflies even have virtually a 360° field of vision, perceiving objects in front of and behind them at the same time. Our vision has its upsides though: we can see in much greater detail than our flying friends.

Looking Pretty Fly

With their iridescent wings, butterflies are the fashionistas of the insect world. Humans have long envied their beautiful colours and we've begun creating technology that copies these creatures.

Shining a light on colour

Light appears white but is actually composed of all the colours of the rainbow. Some butterfly wings have scale-like ridges that force light to bend around them and separate into different colours in a process called diffraction.

These colours 'interfere' with one another. A few meet and become brighter while the rest cancel each other out. This is why butterfly wings sometimes appear to change colour if seen from different angles.

If butterflies are trapped in a spider web, their wing scales detach to help them escape!

Close-up of a butterfly's wing

Did you know?

Unlike humans, butterflies perceive ultraviolet light. When butterflies look at their own wings, they see patterns that are invisible to us but that are very blurry!

Human-eye view

Butterfly-eye view

Winging it

In America, designers have created special screens for electronic devices, which bend light like butterfly wings. These screens are easy to see since external light is harnessed instead of left to cause glare.

Colour me excited!

Certain paints and fabrics have been developed with similar ridges to butterfly wings so that they appear to change colour. This technology doesn't just look cool – dye-free clothes would be better for the environment too.

Black rose

Morphotex dress

Warming to the idea

The black rose butterfly has the potential to revolutionise eco-friendly energy production. This insect is good at absorbing light and heat because of its wing scale structure. Copying these butterflies could help solar panels absorb twice as much of the Sun's energy.

27

Survival Instincts

Animals and plants are pretty tough – to survive as a species for millions of years, you need to be! As we test our own limits, we can borrow from the natural world.

Bird-brained

Some varieties of woodpecker slam their beaks against trees up to 12,000 times a day. They do so to look for food, communicate with each other and carve out nest space.

Skeleton

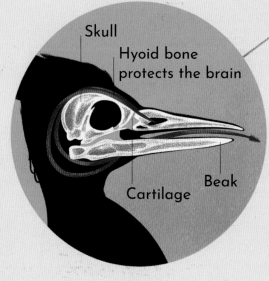

Skull

Hyoid bone protects the brain

Cartilage

Beak

Nature's head-bangers

Woodpeckers withstand colossal impact by having separate beak and skull bones, unlike most other birds. A spongy tissue called cartilage connects the woodpecker's beak and skull and absorbs a lot of the impact when it starts pecking.

Copying woodpecker cartilage, scientists have made bicycle helmets that absorb shock with a layer of cardboard beneath the exterior. This protective gear can absorb three times as much force as polystyrene-layered helmets.

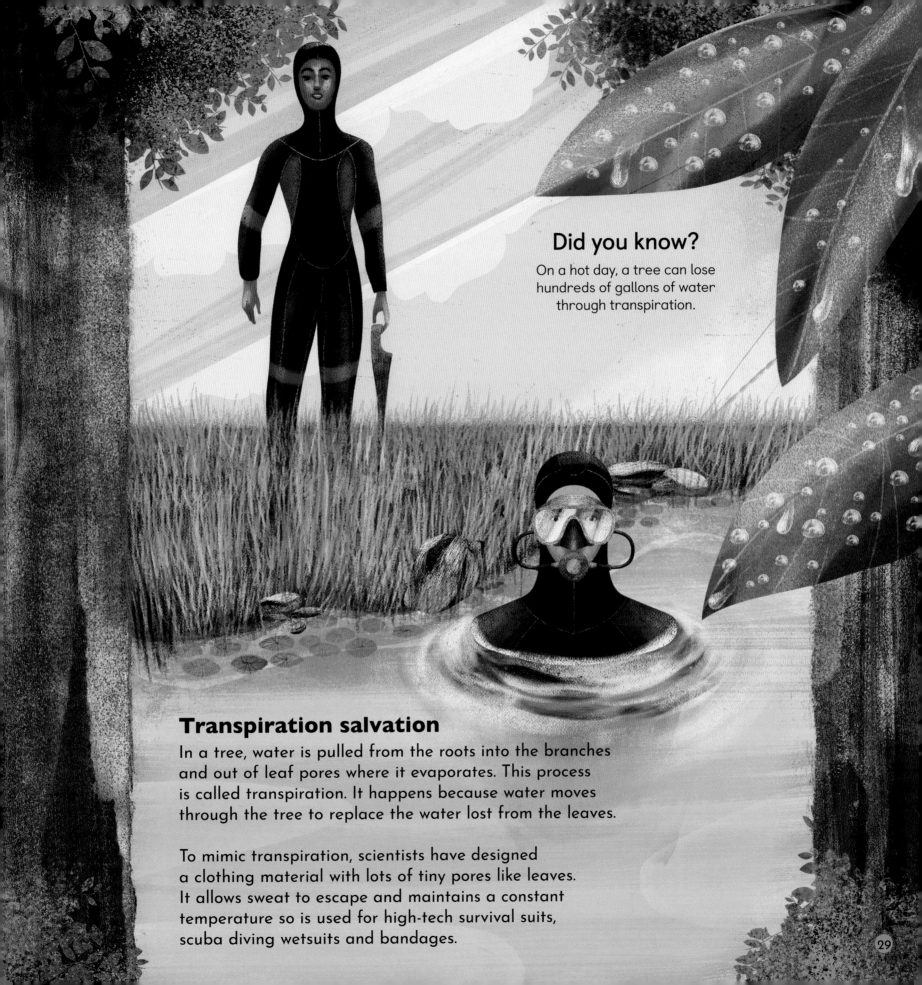

Transpiration salvation

In a tree, water is pulled from the roots into the branches and out of leaf pores where it evaporates. This process is called transpiration. It happens because water moves through the tree to replace the water lost from the leaves.

To mimic transpiration, scientists have designed a clothing material with lots of tiny pores like leaves. It allows sweat to escape and maintains a constant temperature so is used for high-tech survival suits, scuba diving wetsuits and bandages.

Bat Nav

Hello, is anyone there... there... there? You might have noticed that words echo when you speak in a large empty space. Bats have an important use for this phenomenon and scientists have copied nature's resounding achievement...

Sounding out

When a bat makes noise, the sound bounces off nearby objects and returns to the bat's ears. By measuring the length of time between making a sound and hearing its echo, a bat can work out where any obstacles are, their size and whether they are moving. This is called echolocation and helps bats navigate and find tasty snacks.

Make some noise

Sonar (short for sound navigation and ranging) is the human-invented version of echolocation. Sound waves are sent out and scientists gather information from the way these waves return and how long it takes. Originally invented to locate icebergs, sonar now helps in discovering mines, mapping the bottom of the ocean and in ultrasound pregnancy scans. It's particularly useful for sea-based activities since sound travels well in water.

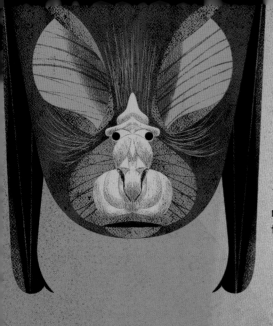

Did you know?

While most bats make noise for echolocation with their tongues or voice boxes, some species, such as the horseshoe bat, use their noses to create sounds. Their nostrils act as mini-megaphones to amplify the noise!

Under the radar

Radio detection and ranging, known as radar, works like echolocation but uses radio waves instead of sound. Radio waves are faster, work better in bad weather and can reach objects further away out of water. Radar's uses include mapping planets and guiding planes.

Big ears

Do you find bats a bit eerie – or should that be ear-y? Bats have large ears to pick up sounds. The horseshoe bat can change the shape of its ears in a tenth of a second to hear better, but bats also contract their ear muscles to protect themselves from their own noise.

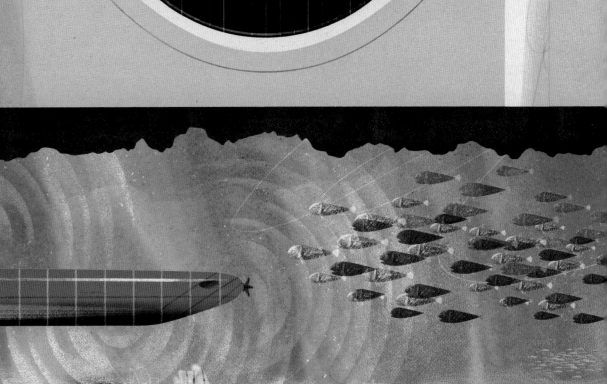

Birds and Bees

Fight or flight, survival of the fittest, it's a dog-eat-dog world. You might think of nature as a competitive arena with species pitted against each other but the wilderness can actually be a place of partnership...

Tiny dancers

It's important that bees can communicate easily because food supply can vary between seasons and even days. When a scout bee discovers a juicy source of nectar, it will let the hive know by dancing! Bees wiggle and waggle to communicate the location, distance and sweetness of the newfound bounty.

To learn this information, the forager bees follow the scout until they have memorised the moves and can find the flowers. After returning, they relay the dance to other bees.

Bird words

In the Turkish settlement of Kuşköy, which translates as 'bird village', shepherds communicate through whistles that can travel across the mountain ranges. Now, locals are more likely to use mobile phones to talk over great distances and only 10,000 whistlers remain.

Sing for your supper

Birds create the most complex sounds found in nature – singing to attract a mate and mark their territory. They can recognise the tunes of different species and make a distinction between the songs of individual birds.

The worldwide hive

Information on the internet is stored by large computers called servers, which connect and send information to the computers you might use at home or school, known as 'clients'. If a lot of 'client' computers are using one server, it can slow down significantly. Just as bees let each other know about work that needs doing, scientists have programmed different servers to 'talk' to each other and share their tasks.

Wood Wide Web

Trees are connected underground by a system of fungi nicknamed 'the wood wide web', otherwise known as the mycelium network. The structure helps trees share nutrients and gases with each other, providing a good example for human communication and exchange.

Family trees

Older and larger trees, or 'mother trees', feed younger ones that can't yet reach the sunlight or grow their roots deep enough into the earth to draw up water. When the mother tree dies it gives away its store of carbon to neighbouring seedlings to provide them with energy. It also sends out defence signals to help prepare smaller trees against future dangers. By looking out for each other in this way, trees can protect their forest.

Tree casual-teas

The umbrella thorn acacia releases a gas when eaten that warns other acacias to put a chemical called tannin into their leaves. People drink tannin in tea and coffee but in large amounts it can be harmful to herbivores.

Giraffes have worked out this tactic though, and munch on leaves upwind where the warning can't reach. Sneaky!

Travel in vein

Leaf veins are the tree's motorways, carrying water and nutrients. Though we usually think that a straight line is the best way to get from A to B, wandering and circular routes are better in the long run. If part of a leaf is damaged, the tree has many ways round the problem. This knowledge could help when planning routes to provide water or electricity to a city.

How to deal with calami-trees

Our world is full of networks: connecting our computers, distributing our electricity and supplying water. As these systems become automated, it's important they have the ability to deal with problems. Trees are cool in a crisis and excellent at helping each other in distress. They can provide a pattern for how such systems handle unexpected disasters.

Coming in to Land...

In this book you've read about some of the ways in which we're trying to root our future in nature. Some of the inventions mentioned can't be made yet on a large scale because they are too expensive or difficult to produce, but researchers are working hard to turn their ideas into reality. One day, your home might be powered by leaf-like solar panels, your lights may glow just like fireflies and you could be wearing clothes based on butterfly wings.

There's still a way to go; more inventions to be made or re-worked. For this, we need people who are entranced by the world around them: who react with the same wonder to the quiet intricacies of leaf veins as to a bullet-fast train; people who look at the smaller details to see the bigger picture. Perhaps we need someone just like you.

Let your imagination run wild.

Glossary of Terms

Abdomen • (Regarding insects) The rear end section of the body.

Air current • Air moving from one place to another.

Air resistance • Force that slows down an object moving through air. It is sometimes called drag.

BASE jump • Jumping with a parachute or wingsuit from a cliff or a high man-made construction.

Bioluminescence • Light naturally given out by a living organism.

Carbon • A chemical element found in carbon dioxide, coal, diamonds and other materials.

Cartilage • Flexible tissue found in the body, especially around joints.

Chlorophyll • Green substance in leaves that absorbs light for photosynthesis.

Clients • (In IT) Computers using a server.

Diffraction • When an obstacle causes light waves to spread out or change direction.

Dougong bracket • Wooden bracket system used in traditional Chinese architecture.

Drag • Force that slows down an object moving through air or liquid.

Drone • Unmanned vehicle that flies.

Echolocation • Method of mapping objects using echoes.

Evaporation • The process of a liquid changing into a gas.

Field of vision • Area that a creature is able to see when its eyes remain fixed on one point.

Force • A push or a pull.

Fossil fuel • Plant or animal remains, including coal or oil, that release energy when burnt.

Frequency • Number of wave cycles per second.

Fungus (plural is fungi) • Plant with no leaves or flowers, such as a mushroom, which feeds on another living organism or decaying material.

Glider • A craft that has no engine and stays up in the air using its own momentum and air currents.

Hertz • Unit to measure sound frequency.

Hyoid bone • A bone that anchors the tongue.

Infrared radiation • A type of energy that we cannnot see but can feel as heat.

Interference • When sound or light waves of the same frequency meet and either cancel each other out or reinforce each other.

Iridescent • When something appears to change colour, depending on the angle from which you look at it.

Larva (plural is larvae) • A young form of an insect or animal, early in its life cycle.

LED • Short for light emitting diode, a light that only allows its electrical current to flow one way.

Lift • Upwards force.

Methane • A gas found in the atmosphere that is released by decaying vegetation and bacteria.

Mycelium network • Fungal system that links trees together so that they can exchange nutrients and information.

Ommatidia • The small components of an insect's eyes.

Ornithopter • Aircraft with flapping wings.

Pagoda • A temple, normally with a tower-like structure.

Pantograph • Mechanical part connecting a vehicle to an overhead wire that provides it with electricity.

Photosynthesis • The process by which a plant gains energy. Carbon dioxide and water are changed into sugar and oxygen using sunlight.

Pitch • How high or low a sound is.

Proboscis • (Regarding insects) The protruding mouth-like body part.

Radar • Stands for radio detection and ranging. A system that locates objects and deduces their speed, position, direction and distance away by bouncing radio waves off them.

Rover • A remote-controlled vehicle that is used to explore difficult terrain.

Server • (In IT) A large computer that holds information for other computers.

Sonar • Stands for sound navigation and ranging. A system that finds objects using sound waves and is often used for locating things underwater.

Stratum corneum • Top layer of skin.

Streamlined • Shaped to move easily through gas or liquid.

Tannin • Yellowy-brown chemical found in plants such as tea.

Thrust • A push force.

Titania • Also known as titanium dioxide. Chemical used in paints, toothpaste and cosmetics.

Transpiration • Movement of water through a plant and out of the leaves where it evaporates.

Ultrasound • Sound with a frequency greater than 20,000Hz, which cannot be heard by humans.

Ultraviolet light • Light that is invisible to humans.

Upwash • Air moving upwards when it meets a wing.

Wavelength • The distance between two identical points on a wave, e.g. from one crest to the next. The difference in wavelength is how we tell different kinds of energy, such as light and sound, apart.

Weight • The downward force caused by gravity affecting an object.